UNITED NATIONS STATISTICAL COMMISSION
and
ECONOMIC COMMISSION FOR EUROPE
CONFERENCE OF EUROPEAN STATISTICIANS

ECONOMIC COMMISSION FOR EUROPE
COMMITEE ON HUMAN SETTLMENTS

STATISTICAL STANDARDS AND STUDIES - No.43

PROGRAMME OF CURRENT HOUSING AND BUILDING STATISTICS FOR COUNTRIES IN THE UN/ECE REGION

UNITED NATIONS
New York, 1993

THE CONFERENCE OF EUROPEAN STATISTICIANS

The Conference of European Statisticians was set up in 1953 as a continuing body meeting under the auspices of the Economic Commission for Europe and the Statistical Commission of the United Nations. Its objectives are *(a)* to improve UN/ECE member countries' official statistics and their international comparability having regard to the recommendations of the Statistical Commission of the United Nations, the specialized agencies and other appropriate bodies as necessary; *(b)* to promote close coordination of the statistical activities in Europe of international organizations so as to achieve greater uniformity in concepts and definitions and to reduce to a minimum the burdens on national statistical offices; and *(c)* to respond to any emerging need for international statistical cooperation arising out of transition, integration and other processes of cooperation both within the UN/ECE region and between it and other regions. The members of the Conference are the directors of the national statistical offices of the countries participating in the work of the United Nations Economic Commission for Europe. The Conference meets in plenary session once a year and also arranges numerous meetings of specialists on particular statistical subjects.

THE COMMITTEE ON HUMAN SETTLEMENTS

The Committee on Human Settlements is one of the Principal Subsidiary Bodies of the United Nations Economic Commission for Europe. It has been active since 1947 as an instrument for intergovernmental cooperation and exchange of experience on problems and policies relating to the planning and development of human settlements. The Committee sponsors studies and investigations and organizes consultations, *ad hoc* meetings and seminars of which those relating to housing and human settlements statistics are convened under the joint auspices of the Committee and the Conference of European Statisticians. Aware of the increasing concern about environmental degradation, particularly in towns and major urban areas, the Committee promotes sustainable development of human settlements. In view of the important social and economic changes that are taking place in central and eastern Europe and the particular problems faced by these countries, the Committee implements activities dealing with key transition issues. To carry out its comprehensive programme of work, the Committee has established the Working Party on Housing Development, Modernization and Management and the Working Party on Sustainable Human Settlements Planning as well as an Expert Group on Human Settlements Problems in southern Europe. The Committee also serves as the focal point for action in the UN/ECE region to implement the recommendations adopted at the United Nations Conference on Human Settlements (Vancouver, 1976). All countries of the region participate on an equal footing in the work of the Committee. Senior policy makers representing ministries responsible for housing, building and regional planning participate in the work of the Committee, which meets once a year.

UNITED NATIONS PUBLICATION
Sales No. E.94.II.E.3
ISBN 92-1-116584-9

RECOMMENDED PROGRAMME OF CURRENT HOUSING AND BUILDING STATISTICS FOR COUNTRIES IN THE UN/ECE REGION

		Table of contents	Paragraphs
CHAPTER I		PURPOSES FOR WHICH CURRENT STATISTICS ON HOUSING AND BUILDING ARE REQUIRED AND THE BROAD TYPES OF STATISTICS NEEDED FOR THESE PURPOSES	1-38
	A.	Statistics on the dwelling stock and changes therein	4-11
	B.	Statistics on the output of housing construction in physical units of measurement	12
	C.	Statistics on conditions of the dwelling stock and expenditure for improvements, repairs and maintenance	13-28
	D.	Statistics on distributional aspects of housing	29-36
	E.	Statistics on house building cost and prices	37-38
CHAPTER II		RECOMMENDED LIST OF STATISTICS	39
CHAPTER III		CONCEPTS, DEFINITIONS AND CLASSIFICATIONS	40-100
	A.	Basic concepts	42-52
	B.	The dwelling stock and changes therein	53-59
	C.	Output of housing construction in physical terms	60-66
		(1) Classification of dwellings completed by type of investor	61
		(2) Classification of dwellings completed by type of equipment	62-63
		(3) Classification of dwellings completed by type of building in which the dwelling is located	64
		(4) Other classifications of dwellings completed	65
		(5) Classifications of dwellings begun or authorized	66
	D.	Conditions of the dwelling stock and data on expenditures for improvements, repairs and maintenance	67-78
	E.	Distributional aspects of housing	79-87
	F.	House building costs and prices	88-100
CHAPTER IV		SOURCES AND METHODS OF COLLECTION	101-117
ANNEX		Recommended tables on distributional aspects of housing	

GE.93-33035

Introduction

The Programme of Current Housing and Building Statistics for countries in the UN/ECE region is a set of statistical standards drawn up in the early 1990s in joint meetings covered by the UN/ECE Committee on Human Settlements and the Conference of European Statisticians. The final text of the Programme was endorsed by the Conference of European Statisticians at its forty-first plenary session (June 1993) and by the Committee on Human Settlements at its fifty-fourth session (September 1993). This programme replaces the earlier one that the Conference and the Committee adopted in the mid 1960s.

The term "Programme" is used in the sense of an agreed statement on a set of statistical series which countries are recommended to collect and publish currently, together with standard definitions and classifications to be applied. The Committee and the Conference recommend that countries endeavour to implement the Programme, or such parts of it as are relevant to their circumstances, in developing their national statistics in this field.

The Programme relates in the first place to statistical series which are of particular international interest and which are or may be published in the statistical publications of UN/ECE, but it is wider in coverage in that it constitutes a framework for the development of national statistics in general, i.e. including statistics which are of national rather than international interest. The Programme has therefore a dual purpose: to assist countries in developing their national statistics on housing and building and to foster international comparability in this field. The Programme should be regarded as a set of long-term objectives to be implemented in stages in accordance with countries' national possibilities, requirements and resources.

The Programme also contains a description and appraisal of the methods most commonly used in compiling the main tyes of statistics covered, but on these questions no specific recommendations are made.

In preparing the Programme the requirements of the Committee on Human Settlements were taken as a starting point. However, experience with the publication of the Annual Bulletin of Housing and Building Statistics for Europe was also taken into account.

The Programme is limited to current statistics, i.e. statistics to be collected and published at least as frequently as annually. It constitutes a supplement to the Recommendations for the 1990 Censuses of Population and Housing in the ECE Region, drawn up by the Conference of European Statisticians and the Committee on Human Settlements, and is consistent with them as regards concepts, definitions and classifications.

The Programme is divided into four chapters. The first chapter discusses the purposes which the respective statistics have to serve and the broad types of statistics required for these purposes. Chapter II lists the statistical series which countries are recommended to collect and publish, together with an indication of the frequency of collection and of the importance attached to different series for international and national purposes respectively. Chapter III sets out the concepts, definitions and classifications recommended in respect of the various subjects. Chapter IV describes the sources and methods most commonly used in collecting and compiling the statistics.

CHAPTER I: PURPOSES FOR WHICH CURRENT STATISTICS ON HOUSING AND BUILDING ARE REQUIRED AND THE BROAD TYPES OF STATISTICS NEEDED FOR THESE PURPOSES

1. In general terms, the purposes which current housing and building statistics have to serve may be described as the provision of data for studies of the situation and trends in the field of housing and for the formulation and implementation of housing policies.

2. For these purposes a broad range of statistics is needed which permits analysis of the size and composition of the dwelling stock and changes therein, the supply of dwellings and factors affecting the supply and demand of dwellings and various factors affecting the demand (rents, housing finance). As housing problems need to be studied and housing policies need to be formulated with due regard to general economic developments and general economic policies, it is necessary that statistics on housing can be directly related and compared with statistics of construction as a whole, and with statistics for other sectors of the economy. While for the formulation of housing requirements and the formulation and implementation of housing policies, data in physical units of measurement are of the greatest importance, for more general analytical and operational purposes and in order to enable the housing situation and trends to be studied in the context of general economic developments, data in value terms (and data on cost, prices, etc.) are also required. Many of the problems encountered in the field of housing are regional problems; it is therefore desirable that at least the main statistical series should be available not only for the country as a whole but also for appropriate territorial sub-divisions (possibly with a classification into urban and rural areas).

3. The present programme covers only part of the statistical requirements described above, namely the requirements for data in physical units of measurement on the housing stock and changes therein and on housing construction. The more specific purposes for which these types of statistics are needed are discussed in some detail below.

A. Statistics on the dwelling stock and changes therein

4. The housing problem continues to be one of the central issues in economic and social policy in most countries of the ECE region. The formulation of housing policies calls for detailed and up to date information on the housing situation and its trends, which permits assessment of the extent of occupation of the housing stock, the size of housing shortages, and present and future housing requirements.

5. The most important sources for this kind of data are the housing censuses, which are periodically taken in nearly all countries of the ECE region. These censures generally provide comprehensive information on the housing stock, its structure and occupancy, including the following data which are particularly relevant to the assessment of the housing structure: a classification of the housing stock by type of housing unit; a classification of dwellings by type of building in which the dwelling is located, by type of installations, by size of the dwelling, by year or period of construction by kind of ownership, and by density of occupation; types and number of households living in dwellings, etc. In most cases, however, it is not feasible to collect such information from censuses on a comprehensive basis more frequently than once every ten years.

6. Similar information, permitting census data to be brought up to date (or information supplementary to census data) is sometimes collected in sample surveys on the housing situation. Such sample surveys, however, are not yet a regular feature of the statistical programmes of all countries. In countries where such surveys are conducted, usually not more than one survey is made between two successive housing censuses. The importance of intercensal sample surveys for up to date assessments of the housing situation for purposes of meeting national policy needs should be stressed.

7.   Information on the housing stock at ten-year intervals is not sufficient to meet the needs of policy makers in the housing field, who need more current information. They also need information at more frequent intervals, such as annually, semi-annually and, in some cases, even quarterly.

8.   The information derived from housing censuses is therefore useful in particular for establishing long-term housing policies. For current policy decisions, these data need to be supplemented by more frequent statistics, available at least annually. Sample surveys, registers and other methods of compiling current statistics are a very important source of information.

9.   For assessing the current housing situation, data are needed in the first place on the dwelling stock. As it is not normally possible to make an inventory of the number of dwellings every year, estimates of the dwelling stock need to be made from data collected at the last census (or survey) and data on current changes in the dwelling stock. Changes in the dwelling stock consist of two elements: (a) increases in the supply of dwellings (i.e. construction of new dwellings, restorations, extensions, conversion of large dwellings into two or more dwellings or of spaces used for non-residential purposes into dwellings); and (b) decreases in the dwelling stock (dwellings becoming unfit for habitation because of deterioration, whether actually demolished or not; dwellings pulled down for reasons other than unfitness for habitation; dwellings destroyed by fire or catastrophes; the conversion of two or more dwellings into a larger dwelling; the conversion of dwellings to non-residential use).

10.   In principle, similar information on the stock of housing units other than conventional dwellings (i.e. semi-permanent housing units, mobile housing units and units not intended for habitation, but in use for the purpose), should also be available since these units are also relevant to the assessment of housing needs and shortage. This information, however, is of much less importance than information relating to conventional dwellings, and is also much more difficult to collect at frequent intervals. The present programme is therefore limited to statistics relating to conventional dwellings.

11.   The dwelling stock and changes therein should be measured not only in terms of the number of dwellings, but also in terms of their size. Two measures by size are relevant, namely the number of rooms per dwelling and the floor space of the dwelling. As the census data, to which current statistics should be related, generally provide information on rooms but not often on the floor space of dwellings, the number of rooms per dwelling will in most cases be the appropriate measure of size.

B.   Statistics on the output of housing construction in physical units of measurement

12.   For the establishment of housing programmes, and for current checking of their implementation, data are needed not only on the total number of dwellings completed, but also on various characteristics of the dwellings added to the dwelling stock and on various factors affecting the trends in dwelling construction. The main requirements are discussed below.

    (a)   The total number of dwellings completed during a given period consists not only of new dwellings constructed but also of additional dwelling units which become available as a result of restoration, extension or conversion of existing dwellings (or other structures). In view of the different significance of these types of building activity for housing programmes and policies, dwellings completed should be analyzed by the type of building activity involved.

    (b)   For assessing short term prospective trends in housing construction, data on the various stages of the work are required. Since new construction is the major component of the total supply of new dwellings and since it usually takes longer to build a new dwelling than to restore, extend or convert one, analysis by stage of work may be confined to new construction of residential buildings. As a minimum, data are required on dwellings completed during the period under review and on dwellings under construction at the end of that period.

(c) For the formulation of housing policies and for checking on their implementation, not only the number of dwellings completed but also the size of the dwellings and the facilities which they provide are of importance. This calls for an analysis by number of rooms and/or floor space, and by type of equipment installed in the dwelling.

(d) An increase in the housing stock depends not only on the technical possibilities of construction, but in many countries also on the ability of the population to pay for the work. A classification of dwellings completed by type of investor is therefore useful.

C. <u>Statistics on the condition of the dwelling stock and expenditures for improvements, repairs and maintenance</u>

13. Data on the condition of the dwelling stock are needed to permit studies of the current quality of the housing inventory, trends in the quality of housing, and for the formulation, implementation and evaluation of housing policies. For these purposes, data are needed which indicate the current state of a unit's liveability. Information should address the state of repair, as well as the presence or absence of basic systems and the suitability of the unit for habitation.

14. In addition to information on the physical state of the structure which would provide basic data on housing quality, for more general analytical and operational purposes, information on the location of poor quality units is also required. Therefore it is desirable that the data be shown not only for the country as a whole but also for different territorial and administrative subdivisions and local areas of special interest.

15. The quantity and quality of the housing stock is an important issue in the economic and social policy of most countries. The formulation of housing policy requires detailed and recent information on the availability of sound units, the number and condition of unfit units, and relative merits of repairing or replacing the substandard structures.

16. Current data series with information on housing quality are limited. Some countries collect information on the condition of the dwelling stock as part of housing censuses which means data are available usually at ten year intervals. The more frequently scheduled household and housing surveys, as well as registers, also may provide some of this information.

17. Data on housing quality should not be limited to occupied dwellings. Vacant structures may provide a reservoir of units available for immediate occupancy or they may need extensive renovation or repairs in order to be utilized. However, practical problems exist with regard to data collection for vacant dwellings.

18. In order to target housing programmes, a count of units by condition and type of ownership, whether public, subsidized, or private, is necessary. Information on the age and type of dwellings is also needed for this purpose.

19. The improvement, repair and maintenance of the housing stock is a large and growing economic activity. Amounts spent increase as the inventory of structures grows and ages. This trend is reinforced by

the diminished likelihood of creating new residential buildings as construction costs, mortgage costs and land prices rise. Land prices increase as the supply of suitable, available land within commuting distance of cities decreases.

20. Statistics on expenditures for improvements, repairs and maintenance are needed to perform economic analysis, including national account statistics. In addition, data for improvements, repairs and maintenance of residential buildings help to create and monitor national housing policy. Data on expenditures for improvements and repairs for the maintenance of residential buildings can be obtained from household surveys, and the information collected from these surveys should distinguish between expenditures on housing repairs and maintenance on the one hand and housing improvements on the other.

21. New construction on the one hand and improvements, repairs and maintenance on the other, are similar processes, however data for these two operations should be available separately. The magnitude of costs for both are likely to be quite dissimilar as are the number of jobs of each type completed. Where possible data for improvements, repairs and maintenance should include all jobs regardless of whether the work was done by the dwelling's occupants or hired labourers.

22. Like the existing data on new construction, information on improvements, repairs and maintenance should be published separately for residential and nonresidential buildings. This is particularly important if the data are to be used in assessing housing condition.

23. In order to monitor housing policies and economic trends efficiently, frequent readings of the housing situation are necessary. Regular sample surveys or compilations from administrative records are recommended to maintain data on residential improvements and repairs.

24. For international purposes, only data at the national level are required. For their own analyses, countries usually need data at the regional level, or in even smaller geographic units.

25. The recommendations in this section deal with the value of improvements, repairs and maintenance made to all buildings, with a distinction between those which are dwellings and those which are nonresidential. For some important housing policy purposes, it is desirable to analyze separately those expenditures made to improve and repair poor quality dwelling units. Furthermore, to help monitor the condition of the dwelling stock, data on the number and type of activities completed in unsound dwellings is useful.

26. In order to evaluate a nation's progress in ameliorating poor living conditions it is not sufficient to monitor data on improvements, maintenance and repairs. Most work of this type is discretionary rather than undertaken to improve unsound dwellings. At a minimum, dwelling quality could be tracked through annual figures on the count of unsound dwellings. However, analysts cannot determine from these data whether unsound dwellings remain in that condition over long or short periods of time, nor whether unsound dwellings are rehabilitated or simply dropped from the housing inventory.

27. Statistics on improvements, repairs and maintenance need to be linked to those on housing quality and tracked over time to determine for example if property owners respond to incentives to repair poor quality dwellings. Longitudinal household or owner surveys which collect information on dwelling quality, on expenditures on improvements, repairs and maintenance and on the types of work completed are an appropriate vehicle. Another worthwhile approach would be integration in one publication of data from several sources, including separate housing and household expenditures surveys, professional housing evaluations, and administrative records.

28.   To do effective evaluation of programs intended to improve dwelling quality and determine future funding needs, more data may be useful. Suggested items include: whether the cost of work on dwellings is paid by private or public funds (show separately occupants' versus other private sources'), the urban/rural location of the units, the type of building (ground-oriented or other), and the cost per job. These data are however of national, rather than international, interest.

D.   Statistics on distributional aspects of housing

29.   In the ECE region there is a growing interest in current international statistics on the housing situation. It is necessary for national and international programs to have internationally comparable figures on the distribution of households over the housing stock. It is also necessary to have comparable figures on improvements or changes in the housing stock. There is a growing interest in the existing housing stock . In the Western European countries and North America the influence of new housing starts is diminishing as a consequence of changing population structures. Of particular importance is the match between the housing stock and persons in the household, etc. In most ECE countries one of the major objectives is to achieve a housing distribution that is sufficient to meet important housing needs in the country.

30.   The costs of housing form a substantial part of the total budget of most households. For this reason it is important to know the diversity of housing costs for various households. This type of information is useful within the context of national policies aimed at redirecting subsidies in relation to the distribution of households over the housing stock. Information on the cost of housing is also important at the international level (e.g. for studies of poverty, income levels, etc.).

31.   The national and international "skewness" in the distribution of households over the housing stock becomes of greater importance with the anticipated greater mobility of the population within the ECE region. Therefore, it is recommended that internationally comparable data should be collected on the distributional aspects of housing. In this respect there are three starting points: (i)Housing size distribution; (ii) Housing expenditures, and (iii) Housing quality, i.e. state of repair, equipment and crowding". The understanding of the situation in countries with different housing market systems (and processes) will benefit from these comparisons. Some illustrations of recommended tables on distributional aspects of housing are given in the Annex.

32.   The following characteristics of the households and housing stock relevant for international comparison could be considered: dwelling size, household size, housing costs, quality aspects and facilities in the dwelling. The information should be organized initially in the form of cross tabulations of housing and households. It is also important to have information about the number of people in the households in relation to the size of the dwelling. The amount of space an individual can use is part of the experienced quality of life.

33.   With respect to housing costs, most countries collect information about annual household expenditures through budget surveys.

34.   The same argument applies for the facilities in the dwelling. The distribution data should not be limited to occupied dwellings but should, as far as possible, also contain data on vacant dwellings as well as on persons/households not living in conventional dwellings.

35.   Ideally, data acquisition should occur in five year intervals. This could be either achieved through surveys or registers. As many ECE countries as possible should be encouraged to acquire and provide the data about the distributional aspects of housing. The objective should also be to have as many countries as possible comply with and use the internationally agreed definitions contained in the recommendations for

the most recent round of population and housing censuses in the ECE region, and to have footnotes in tabulations only in cases where countries do not follow the recommendations and/or do not produce estimates that adjust the national data to the international standard;

36.   Existing variables within the *Programme* and the *Annual Bulletin of Housing and Building Statistics for Europe* for describing the dwelling stock and the households should be used as much as possible to maximise the likelihood that these variables may be fully cross-tabulated.

E.   Statistics on house building cost and prices

37.   The reason for gathering statistics on building cost and prices is the sustained interest in the volume of expenditure devoted annually to the construction of new dwellings, to the replacement of obsolete dwellings and the maintenance of the existing dwelling stock. Considerable governmental expenditures on financing of housing programmes drew attention to the means of reducing house building costs. It is obvious that any systematic effort to reduce building costs must be based in the first instance on reliable statistical information.

38.   It is important to get information on the current market price of dwellings and the prices that tenants/owners pay in relation to income levels.

CHAPTER II: RECOMMENDED LIST OF STATISTICS

39.   The list of statistics which countries are recommended to compile and publish are set out below. In connection with this list the following points should be noted:

(a)   The list is limited to the types of statistics which are regarded as of interest to most countries; statistics which are likely to be of interest only in special national circumstances are not included. With a few exceptions "derived" statistics such as per capita data or average size of dwellings are not included.

(b)   In the list, a distinction is made between two categories of statistics: statistics which are important internationally and which countries should endeavour to provide (referred to as category 1); and statistics which are primarily of interest for national purposes (referred to as category 2).

(c)   The recommendations concerning periodicity in respect of statistics in category 1 reflect international needs; for national purposes the statistics may be required more frequently.

(d)   Definitions and standard classifications for all items included in category 1, and in some cases for those included in category 2 (the cases where it appears desirable and possible to give guidance to countries wishing to compile the statistics in question) are given in Chapter III of this Programme. In that chapter, reference is also made in some cases to some further classifications of data, which countries may find useful for various purposes, but for which, in view of divergences in national requirements, it is not feasible to make specific recommendations.

Description of statistical series	Periodicity	Category

I.   **STATISTICS ON THE DWELLING STOCK AND CHANGES THEREIN**

1.   **Increases in the dwelling stock**

(a) Total increases	A	1
of which: new construction	A	1

(b)   Classification by geographical location
   (i) urban areas
  (ii) rural areas
	A	2

(c) Classification by size of dwelling (by number of rooms per dwelling)	A	2

2.   **Decreases in the dwelling stock**

(a)   Total decreases
 	
   (i) resulting from demolition
  (ii) resulting from change in use
	A	1

(b)   Classification by geographical location
 	
   (i) urban areas
  (ii) rural areas
	A	2

(c) Classification by size of dwelling (by number of rooms per dwelling)	A	2

3.   **Dwelling stock**

(a) Total dwelling stock	A	1

(b)   Classification by geographical location
   (i) urban areas
  (ii) rural areas
	A	2

Description of statistical series	Periodicity	Category
(c) Classification by size of dwelling (by number of rooms per dwelling)	A	2
(d) Classification by period of construction	A	1
(i) before 1919		
(ii) 1919-1945		
(iii) 1946-1960		
(iv) 1961-1970		
(v) 1971-1980		
(vi) 1981-1985		
(vii) 1986-1990		
(viii) 1991 and later		
(e) Classification on equipment of dwellings	A	1
(i) piped water within the dwelling		
(ii) fixed bath or shower within the dwelling		
(iii) flush toilet within the dwelling		
(iv) central heating		
(v) electricity	A	2
(vi) Type of sewage disposal system	A	2
(vii) Piped gas	A	2
(viii) Telephone	A	2
(f) Classification on availability of a kitchen	A	1
(i) with a kitchen		
(ii) with a kitchenette (that is a separate space with less than 4 sq. metres or two metres width of floorspace)		
(iii) without a kitchen or kitchenette		

II.   **STATISTICS ON THE OUTPUT OF HOUSING CONSTRUCTION IN PHYSICAL UNITS OF MEASUREMENT**

1.   **Stages of building work - new construction of residential buildings only**

Description of statistical series	Periodicity	Category
(a) Dwellings authorized during the year	Q	2
(b) Dwellings begun during the year	Q	2
(c) Dwellings under construction at year end	Q	1
(d) Dwellings completed	Q	1
2. Number and size of dwellings completed by all building activities		
(a) Total number of dwellings	Q	1
(b) Total number of rooms	A	1
(c) Useful floor space (sq. m.)	A	1
(d) Living floor space (sq. m.)	A	2
3. Classification of dwellings completed by all building activities, by		
(a) Type of building activity	A	1
(i) new construction		
(ii) other building activity, of which:		
- restorations	A	2
- extensions	A	2
- conversions	A	2
(b) Size of dwellings (number of rooms)	A	1
Periodicity Category		
(c) Type of investor	A	1
(i) state and local governments		
(ii) other public bodies		
(iii) housing cooperatives		
(iv) private bodies		
(v) private persons		
(d) Type of equipment	A	1
(i) piped water		
(ii) fixed bath or shower		

Description of statistical series	Periodicity	Category

(iii) central heating

(e) Geographical location   A   2
   (i) urban areas
   (ii) rural areas

4. <u>Classification of dwellings completed by new construction, by type of building in which dwellings are located</u>

   (i) dwellings in ground-oriented   A   1
      residential buildings (1000)

      of which in: one-dwelling buildings
      (Percentages)

      two-dwelling buildings
      (Percentages)

      three or more dwelling
      buildings (Percentages)

   (ii) dwellings in other   A   1
       residential
       buildings (1000)
       of which with: 1 or 2 stories
         (Percentages)
         3 to 5 stories
         (Percentages)

         6 to 8 stories
         (Percentages)

         9 stories and over
         (Percentages)

   (iii) dwellings in non-residential   A   1
       buildings (1000)

III. STATISTICS ON THE CONDITION
OF THE DWELLING STOCK AND
VALUE OF CONSTRUCTION PUT
IN PLACE (INCLUDING DATA ON
EXPENDITURES FOR IMPROVEMENTS,
REPAIRS AND MAINTENANCE)

Description of statistical series	Periodicity	Category

1. Condition of the dwelling stock

In order to produce statistics on housing condition, an extensive series of questions are needed. The data from individual items are not recommended for international publication with a few exceptions. These are: the percentage of dwellings with electricity; the percentage of dwellings with toilet facilities; and the percentage of dwellings with cooking facilities. The recommendations for collection periodicity for category 1 statistics reflects international needs; for national purposes this data may be required more frequently.

(a) Number of unsound dwellings (1000 dwellings) lacking 1 or more items of equipment (Percentages)	A	1
- with inadequate equipment (Percentages)		
- with 1 or more structural defects (Percentages)		
(b) Tenure of dwellings:	A	1
- owner-occupied, of which, percent unsound		
- renter-occupied, of which, percent unsound		
(c) Ownership of dwellings:	A	2
- private, of which percent unsound		
- public, of which, percent unsound		

2. Value of construction put in place (including data on expenditures for improvements, repairs and maintenance

Description of statistical series	Periodicity	Category

The list of statistics recommended for compilation and publication appears below. The recommendations for collection periodicity for category 1 statistics reflect international needs; for national purposes this data may be required more frequently.

Total Construction (in national currency)

(i) New construction and improvements	A	1
(ii) Maintenance and repairs	A	1

Residential Construction

(a) new construction	A	1
(b) improvements	A	1
(c) repairs and maintenance	A	1

Non-residential Construction

(i) New buildings and improvements	A	1
- New buildings	A	1
- Improvements	A	1
(ii) Civil engineering (new and improvements)	A	1
(iii) Maintenance and repairs	A	1

V.   DISTRIBUTIONAL ASPECTS OF HOUSING

It is important and useful for countries to collect statistics on distributional aspects of housing. At this stage, some latitude is left to countries in deciding what types of statistics to develop, pending further progress being made by them.

1.   The following statistics are recommended to be compiled:

(a) Number of dwellings and rooms in dwellings	A	1

Description of statistical series	Periodicity	Category
(b) Number of households and persons in households	A	1
(c) Number of overcrowded dwellings (with 1.5 and more persons per room)	A	1
(d) Useful floor space	A	1
(e) Living floor space	A	1
(f) Non-availability of facilities	A	1
(g) Tenure status	A	1

- Countries may wish to collect information on the useful floor space and/or on the living floor space of dwellings.

- It is suggested that overcrowded be defined as more than 1.5 persons per room. Some countries may wish to set a lower or higher standard based on national experience (possible ranges could be 0.5-2.0 occupants per room).

2.   First priority should be place on the cross-tabulations listed below. Second priority tables could deal with variables such as income, socio-economic group and type of household.

3.   The tables recommended for the first stage are as follows:

(a) Number of rooms in a dwelling, number of persons in a household, average size of household;

(b) Number of persons in a household, useful floor space by tenure;

(c) Number of persons in a household, living floor space by tenure;

(d) Number of rooms in a dwelling, number of persons in a household, total number of households, by tenure;

(e) Number of rooms in a dwelling by useful floor space;

(f) Number of rooms in a dwelling by living floor space;

(g) Number of rooms in a dwelling and absence of facilities, by tenure;

(h) Number of persons in a household and absence of facilities, by tenure.

These tables are listed in the Annex.

Description of statistical series	Periodicity	Category

4.   It is important to have information on housing expenditures for various types of households. However, the concept and definitions of income on the one hand and housing consumption on the other differ to such an extent that internationally comparable information (other than macro expenditure/income ratios) are not available at present. Countries are recommended to develop as much information as possible on household expenditures for various classifications of households and dwellings. They should use internationally agreed concepts of income and housing expenditures. There are different methods to describe household expenditures. For purposes of measuring the annual consumption of housing services the concept of the "out of pocket" method seems appropriate. However, for purposes of international comparisons of household expenditures and for purposes of comparing tenure status, the rent equivalence concept may be appropriate. The "out of pocket" concept describes the annual expenditures made by a household for the use of the dwelling and related services. The rent equivalence method uses a concept in which the owner-occupier is treated as if he is renting his dwelling. By this method expenditures which are done more incidentally or are the result of buying the dwelling (.e.g. the loss of the profit from savings) are included in the expenditure/income ratio on a household level.

V.   HOUSE BUILDING COST AND PRICES

1.   In connection with the list of statistics set out below which countries are recommended to compile and publish, the following points should be noted:

   (a) annual periodicity is recommended for these types of statistics

   (b) the statistics should be collected and published for selected groups or types of residential buildings, which are uniform within each group from the point of view of size, equipment and technology used in construction.

1. Statistics to be gathered

(a) Costs or prices	A	1
(b) Useful floor space (sq. m.)	A	1
(c) Number of dwellings	A	1
(d) Gross volume of buildings (cu.m.)	A	2

2.   Statistics to be published

Average costs or price per:

(a) Dwelling	A	1
(b) Sq. m. of useful floor space	A	1

(c) Cu. m. of gross volume of
        residential
        buildings
	A	2

CHAPTER III: CONCEPTS, DEFINITIONS AND CLASSIFICATIONS

40.   The basic concepts applying to the statistics covered by the Programme are set out in section A below. Concepts, definitions and classifications relating to the specific topics covered by the Programme are given in the following sections of this chapter.

41.   The actual definitions used in national statistics are to a certain extent affected by the methods by which the data are obtained. In some cases deviations from the standard definitions set out below may therefore occur. When this is the case, countries are recommended to indicate in their publications the differences between the national and international definitions.

A.   Basic Concepts

Building

42.   A building is any independent structure containing one or more dwellings, rooms or other spaces, covered by a roof and enclosed within external walls or dividing walls which extend from the foundations to the roof, whether designed for residential or for agricultural, commercial, industrial or cultural purposes or for the provision of services.

Residential and non-residential buildings

43.   A building should be regarded as residential when the major part of the building (i.e. more than half of its gross floor area) is used for dwelling purposes. Other buildings should be regarded as non-residential.

Dwelling stock

44.   The dwelling stock includes only conventional (permanent) dwellings (e.g. a house, apartment, room or suite of rooms), whether occupied or not. The simple term "dwelling" is generally used instead of "conventional dwelling". The dwelling stock does not include rustic (semi-permanent) and improvised housing units (e.g. huts, cabins, shanties), mobile housing units (e.g. trailers, caravans, tents, wagons, boats) and housing units not intended for human habitation but in temporary use for the purpose (e.g. stables, barns, mills, garages, warehouses).

Conventional dwelling

45.   A conventional dwelling is a room or suite of rooms and its accessories (e.g. lobbies, corridors) in a permanent building or structurally separated part thereof which by the way it has been built, rebuilt or converted is designed for habitation by one private household all the year round and is not at the time of the census used wholly for non-residential purposes. It should have separate access to the street, direct or via a garden or grounds, or to a common space within the building (staircase, passage, gallery, etc.), but it need not necessarily have a bathroom or toilet available for the exclusive use of its occupants. A "permanent building" is one which was constructed to be structurally stable for at least ten years, but some countries may wish to define permanence instead in terms of the method of construction or in terms of the building materials used. Detached rooms for habitation which are clearly designed to be used as part of the dwelling should be included, e.g. a room or rooms above a detached garage.

Room

46.   A room is defined as a space in a dwelling enclosed by walls reaching from the floor to the ceiling or roof covering, or at least to a height of 2 metres above the ground, of a size large enough to hold a bed

for an adult (4 square metres at least) and at least 2 metres high over the major area of the ceiling. Thus, normal bedrooms, dining rooms, living rooms, habitable cellars and attics, servants' rooms, kitchens and other separate spaces used or intended for habitation all count as rooms. A kitchenette (i.e. a kitchen of less than 4 square metres or 2 metres wide), corridors, verandas, utility rooms (e.g. boiler rooms, laundry rooms) and lobbies do not count as rooms, nor do bathrooms and toilets (even if they are more than 4 square metres).

Floor space of a dwelling

47.   Two concepts of floor space of a dwelling are used:

   (a) Useful floor space is the floor space of dwellings measured inside the outer walls, excluding non-habitable cellars, attics and, in multi-dwelling houses, all common spaces;

   (b) Living floor space is the total floor space of rooms falling under the concept of "room" as defined in paragraph 46.

Types of building activity

48.   In residential construction, three types of building activity are distinguished: new construction; improvements; repairs and maintenance. They are defined as follows:

   (a) New construction means the erection of an entirely new structure, whether or not the site on which it is built was previously occupied;

   (b) Improvements - construction work by which the utility of dwellings is increased or at least renewed (i.e. by work which materially extends the normal life of those fixed assets) and where the value of the dwellings is increased. Improvements on property outside dwellings is also included. Restorations, extensions and conversions should be included here.

      (i) Restoration means repairs by which at least one dwelling or other structure is effectively reinstated and where substantial parts of the existing structure are used;

      (ii) Extension relates to the enlargement of buildings by which space is added. Examples are adding room(s), raising a roof or digging a basement.

      (iii) Conversion relates to structural changes carried out within a building. In statistics relating to changes in the dwelling stock, only those extensions and conversions are taken into account which result in an increase or decrease of the number of dwellings.

   (c) Repairs and maintenance - construction work which does not, in principle, result in extending the normal life of dwellings, but only prevents their abnormal deterioration, keeps them in a state of normal functioning and maintains their value.

Stages of construction work

49.   The following stages of work are distinguished:

(a) <u>Work authorized</u> - building projects for the carrying out of which a permit has been issued.

(b) <u>Work begun</u> - work is begun when the first physical operations are undertaken on the construction site after the planning and designing stage, i.e. depending on national practices: the preparation of the site; the delivery of materials and equipment to the site; the start of excavations; or the laying of foundations.

(c) <u>Work under construction</u> - work begun but not yet completed.

(d) <u>Work completed</u> - work is completed when the building or other structure is physically ready to be occupied or to be put into use.

In some countries data on work authorized are published as a substitute for data on work begun. In these cases it is desirable that an indication be provided of the approximate proportion of building permits which result in actual building work.

<u>Geographical location</u>

50. There are no standard, internationally recommended definitions of urban and rural areas. Since current statistics are needed to bring up to date the data on the dwelling stock obtained in housing censuses, countries are recommended to use the same urban/rural classification as adopted in their most recent housing census. It is suggested that for purposes of international comparisons, countries define <u>urban areas</u> as localities with a population of 2,000 or more, and <u>rural areas</u> as localities with a population of less than 2,000 and sparsely populated areas. Some countries might also wish to consider defining urban areas in other ways (e.g. in terms of administrative boundaries, of built-up areas, of the area for which services such as shops, educational facilities, recreational facilities, employment, etc., are provided, or in terms of functional areas). Countries are also recommended to indicate in their statistical publications the definitions of urban and rural areas used.

51. In addition to an urban/rural classification, a classification by region or by size of community is likely to be useful for national purposes.

<u>Dwellings by type of ownership</u>

52. The following classification of dwellings by type of ownership is recommended:

(a) Owner-occupied dwellings - This category includes all dwellings which are used wholly or partly for own occupation by the owner.

(b) Other dwellings
- In private ownership
- In other types of ownership.

B. <u>The dwelling stock and changes therein</u>

53. <u>Increases in the dwelling stock</u> include increases in the number of dwellings due to new construction and increases due to other types of building activity (restoration, extension, conversion). In principle, increases in the number of dwellings without building activity (conversion of one dwelling into two or more dwellings, or of space used for non-residential purposes into one or more dwellings without building activity)

should also be taken into account, but increases due to these factors are likely to be of little quantitative importance. The definitions of new construction, restoration, extension and conversion are given in paragraph 45.

54.   Decreases in the dwelling stock consist of the following components: a) dwellings becoming definitely empty (e.g. because they are declared unsound for habitation or because it is evident that they will not again be occupied permanently), whether demolished or not, included in this category are also dwellings which, after having become unsound for habitation, are subsequently restored and effectively reinstated (as indicated above, the restoration of the dwelling should be recorded as an increase in the dwelling stock); b) dwellings sound for habitation but demolished, e.g. to make way for the construction or extension of factories, the construction of new roads or the widening of existing roads; c) dwellings destroyed by fire, floods, subsidence or other catastrophes; d) decreases in the number of dwellings resulting in the conversion of two or more dwellings into one dwelling or of one or more dwellings into non-residential accommodation (with or without building activity).

55.   In order to permit classification of the dwelling stock and changes therein by the size of the dwellings, it is recommended that changes in the number of dwellings due to conversions be recorded on a "gross" basis, i.e. that the total number of dwellings that have been converted be recorded as a decrease in the dwelling stock; and that the total number of dwellings resulting from the conversion be recorded as an increase in the dwelling stock.

56.   If the dwelling stock is to be measured not only in terms of the number of dwellings but also in terms of their size, account should in principle be taken also of those extensions and conversions which result in an increase of the size, though not of the number of dwellings. The magnitudes involved are, however, likely to be of minor importance, and it is therefore not proposed that they should be recorded.

57.   When all increases and decreases are currently recorded, it will be relatively easy to keep up to date the statistics on the size of the dwelling stock obtained in housing censuses. In cases where only partial data on decreases are available, it is recommended that, if possible, the missing data be estimated so as to enable at least approximate measures of the total dwelling stock to be compiled currently.

58.   With regard to the classification of the dwelling stock and changes therein by size of the dwelling (number of rooms), it is recommended that separate size classes be provided for dwellings of different sizes (i.e. 1, 2, 3, 4, etc. rooms per dwelling, and not 1 or 2 rooms, 3 or 4 rooms per dwelling). It is left to individual countries to decide on the number of size classes to be shown, but the classification should be sufficiently detailed that the largest size class included does not cover more than ten per cent of the total dwelling stock.

59.   Countries which exclude kitchens from the count of rooms are recommended to make available separate data (or estimates) on the approximate number of kitchens so excluded.

C.   Output of housing construction in physical terms

60.   The recommended list of statistics provides for two basic classifications of the output of housing construction in physical terms: first, a distinction by type of building activity (new construction; improvements; repairs and maintenance); and second, in respect of new construction, a classification by stage of construction work (work authorized, work begun, work under construction, work completed). As regards improvements, repairs and maintenance, the only compilation recommended is of dwellings completed, since data on work begun and work under construction in respect of these types of activity are regarded as of lesser importance. The definitions of the different types of building activity and of the stages of construction

work are given in Section A of this chapter. The other classifications of output of housing construction recommended in the Programme are considered below.

(1)   Classification of dwellings completed by type of investor

61.   This classification applies to dwellings completed by all types of building activity. The term "investor" refers to the bodies or persons on whose account of dwellings are built (irrespective of whether or not they are owners of the land on which the dwellings are built) and not to those actually erecting them. The most detailed categories of type of investor needed for national purposes are likely to vary between countries according to their social and institutional arrangements. For international purposes, however, categories of national classifications should be converted into the following broader headings:

State and local governments - This category includes both central governmental bodies and governmental bodies on all lower levels (provinces, regions, counties, municipalities).

Other public bodies - These should be defined mainly on the basis of their function and not of their legal status which may be the same or similar to that of private bodies. However, the functions which these bodies exercise should have public aspects. In principle, they are non-profit making organizations providing low-cost housing, and usually operate under special legislation.

Private persons - In this category should fall all individuals undertaking house building for own occupation or for renting and also for possible sale.

Co-operatives - The main function of housing co-operatives is usually to provide their members with accommodation mostly by way of house-building. In principle, housing co-operatives have a non-profit making character and operate exclusively for the benefit of their members. The members make a personal contribution, generally in cash. Housing co-operatives do, of course, make use for house building purposes of various types of financial assistance, from public authorities, specialized credit organizations and social organizations.

Other private bodies - This category includes, in principle, organizations operating on a profit-making basis, e.g. private enterprises of any kind, real estate agents. They may provide accommodation for their employees or build houses for renting or sale.

(2)   Classification of dwellings completed by type of equipment

62.   This classification also covers dwellings completed by all types of building activity.

63.   The classifications by type of equipment recommended in the programme are limited to those kinds of facility which are regarded as of interest to most countries. No classifications are proposed in respect of facilities which are likely to be included in nearly all dwellings in countries of the ECE region, such as electricity or toilet installations. The definitions of the various types of equipment distinguished in the classifications are as follows:

(a) Piped water - Dwellings are regarded as equipped with piped water if it is laid on inside the dwelling. Piped water may be provided either from a community scheme or from a private installation.

(b) Fixed bath or shower - Dwellings are counted as equipped with fixed bath or shower if at least one of these types of equipment is installed inside the dwelling.

(c) <u>Central heating</u> - Dwellings are considered as centrally heated if heating is provided either from a community heating centre or from an installation built in the building or in the dwelling, established for heating purposes, without regard to the source of energy.

(d) <u>Telephone</u> - available in the dwelling

(e) <u>Type of sewage disposal system</u>

    (i) Toilet empties into a piped system connected to a public sewage disposal plant.

    (ii) Toilet empties into a piped system connected to a private sewage disposal plant (e.g. a septic tank built for a single housing unit or a small group of housing units).

    (iii) All other arrangements (e.g. toilet empties into an open ditch, a pit, a cesspool, a river, the sea, etc.)

(f) <u>Piped gas</u> - available in the dwelling

(g) <u>Electricity</u> - available in the dwelling

(3) <u>Classification of dwellings completed by type of building in which the dwelling is located</u>

64. This classification is limited to new dwellings completed. The headings of the recommended classification are defined as follows:

- **Ground-oriented residential buildings** - This category includes all types of houses (detached, semi-detached, terraced houses, houses built in a row, etc.) each dwelling of which has its own entrance directly from the ground surface.

- **Other residential buildings** - This category includes all residential buildings other than ground-oriented residential buildings as defined above. Residential buildings are sub-divided according to the number of stories of the building. For this purpose, all floors above ground level (including the ground floor) are counted as stories. Floors below ground and attics should be disregarded.

- **Non-residential buildings** - Definitions of residential and non-residential buildings are given in para.43.

(4) <u>Other classifications of dwellings completed</u>

65. The Programme also provides for classifications of dwellings completed by size of dwellings and by geographical location. As regards the classifications to be used for these purposes, see paragraphs 50 and 58 above.

(5) <u>Classifications of dwellings begun or authorized</u>

66. All classifications recommended in the Programme relate to dwellings completed (or dwellings completed by new construction). In a number of countries it may not yet be possible to collect the information required in respect of dwellings completed. If in these countries the necessary data are available in respect of dwellings begun or authorized, it is recommended that the proposed classifications be compiled on that basis. While classifications of dwellings begun or authorized differ from those of dwellings completed (<u>inter alia</u> because most dwellings begun or authorized during a given period are not completed

during that period), they may nevertheless provide a useful though approximate picture of the various aspects of the development of housing construction.

D.   Condition of the dwelling stock and data on expenditure for improvements and repairs
       Condition of the dwelling stock

67.   All concepts for these types of statistics are defined below.

68.   The actual definitions used in national statistics are to some extent affected by the methods by which the data are obtained, therefore some deviations from these standards may occur. When this is the case, countries are recommended to indicate in their publications the differences between the national and international definitions.

69.   The condition of the dwelling stock is a judgement based on two main factors:

-     the physical state of repair of the dwelling;
-     the availability and adequacy of specific equipment for the dwelling.

70.   A third factor is the size of the dwelling in relation to its number of occupants (which is also an element of housing distribution aspects). The data recommended for collection under this programme are intended to allow countries to designate units as "sound" or unsound". Dwellings which fail to meet minimal standards in relation to the designated factors are deemed 'unsound'.

71.   "A dwelling is considered to be lacking equipment if it is missing one or more of the following items of required equipment in working order or if the equipment does not meet the needs of the occupants:

(a) piped water within the dwelling;

(b) fixed bath or shower within the dwelling;

(c) flush toilet within the dwelling;

(d) kitchen or kitchenette within the dwelling;

(e) heating facilities;

(f) electricity available in the dwelling.

Electricity

72.   Dwellings are considered as having electricity if they are connected to a source which regularly provides electric power 24 hours a day. The source may be a power grid or an individual generator.

Toilet facilities

73.   For data on housing condition, only dwellings with a flush toilet within the dwelling are defined as having toilet facilities.

Inadequate equipment

74.   Equipment are considered inadequate if they do not regularly and effectively perform their function. The items of equipment to which this definition is applied are: piped water; fixed bath or shower; flush

toilet; kitchen or kitchenette; heating facilities; and electricity (all items of equipment available within the dwelling).

Cross-classification of type of equipment and age of dwelling

75.   It can also be useful to have a cross-classification of dwellings by period of construction and availability of equipment and facilities.

Structural defects

76.   A structural defect could be (but need not be limited to) a fault in the original construction or the current maintenance of the dwelling which endangers the health or safety of its occupants or its neighbours. Defects are categorized by the six parts of the structure at fault: foundation, walls, roof, floors, stairways, and exterior openings (windows and doors). A dwelling is considered to have a structural defect if it has at least one serious problem in any of its six components; or if it has two or more moderate problems its six components. Defects in the basic frame are considered to be serious defects. Illustrations on possible serious and moderate defects are as follows:

Serious Defects:

Roof   (i)   missing covering materials (such as shingles, tiles, etc.) or holes in the roof, or

      (ii)   chimney off-plumb or bulging

Walls   (i)   exterior walls allow the dwelling's interior to be exposed to the elements (by means of holes, cracks, or gaps), or

      (ii)   interior walls off-plumb

Exterior openings coverings (doors or windows) missing

Stairways missing, crumbled or rotted steps

Floors with holes, or sagging or rotted areas

Foundation sections missing, bulging, sagging, or off-plumb.

Moderate Defects

Roof   (i) missing gutters (where normally used), or

      (ii) permits water to leak into the dwelling

Walls   Interior walls have large areas of broken plaster, peeling paint, or mould

Exterior openings coverings (doors or windows) allow entry of elements to dwelling's interior (broken, rotted, warped, etc.)

Stairways   (i) no secure handrailings, or

(ii) no artificial lighting

Foundation admits entry of moisture to dwelling's interior.

Occupants per room

77.   This is a derived statistic based on the number of persons whose usual place of residence is the dwelling divided by the number of rooms in the dwelling. It is an aspect of housing distribution which is useful to relate to information on housing conditions. It provides a measure of the amount of crowding in the dwelling. Dwellings which otherwise have all equipment and are in good physical condition may still be inadequate for the needs of the occupants based on the number of persons sharing the same living space. It is suggested that overcrowded is defined as more than 1.5 persons per room. Some countries may wish to set lower or higher standards based on national experience (possible ranges could be 0,5 - 2.0 occupants per room).

Expenditures for improvements, repairs and maintenance

78.   All concepts for these statistics are defined in para.48.

E.   Distributional aspects of housing

79.   The definitions proposed for use in describing distributional aspects of housing are presented below:

Household

80.   There are two concepts of household: one is based on the housekeeping unit concept and another on the household dwelling concept.

81.   The housekeeping unit concept specifies a private household as either:

(a) a one-person household, i.e. a person who lives alone in a separate housing unit or who occupies, as a lodger, a separate room (or rooms) of a housing unit but does not join with any of the other occupants of the housing unit to form part of a multi-person household as defined below; or

(b) a multi-person household, i.e. a group of two or more persons who combine to occupy the whole or part of a housing unit and to provide themselves with food and possibly other essentials for living. The group may pool their income to a greater or lesser extent. The group may be composed of related persons only or of unrelated persons or of a combination of both, including boarders and excluding lodgers.

82.   In the household-dwelling concept the private household is equated with the housing unit. It does not provide direct information on the number of housekeeping units sharing housing units. It is recommended that countries applying the household-dwelling concept give an estimate of the total number of housekeeping units in the census report. If the difference between the number of household-dwelling units and the number of housekeeping units is significant, these countries should also endeavour to analyze the occupants of housing units in such a way that they are able to compile the recommended basic tabulations relating to private households on the basis of the housekeeping unit concept as well.

83.   Countries should specify in their census reports whether they used the housekeeping unit or the household-dwelling concept of a private household.

Average size of household

84.   The ratio of population living in households to number of households. Persons not living in households (for example, in military barracks) are excluded.

Reference person of private household

85.   Information should be collected for all persons living in private households on their relationship to the reference member of the household. Data on this topic are needed for use in (i) identifying households and family nuclei; and (ii) compiling tabulations in which households are classified according to characteristics of the reference member. It is left to countries to decide whether the reference member should be:

(a)   the head of household;

(b)   the head of household or one of the joint heads;

(c)   the person (or one of the persons) who owns or rents the housing unit or in whose name the housing unit is occupied under some other form of tenure or in whose name part of the housing unit is rented or occupied under some other form of tenure;

(d)   an adult person selected with a view to facilitating the determination of family relationships; or

(e)   a person selected on the basis of other criteria.

It is important that countries describe clearly in the census report the concept of the reference member that has been adopted and the definition that has been used.

Number of occupants

86.   Each person usually resident in a housing unit or other living quarters should be counted as an occupant of those living quarters. However, since housing censuses are usually carried out simultaneously with population censuses, the possibility of applying this definition depends upon whether the information collected and recorded for each person in the population census indicates where he spent the census night or whether it refers to his place of usual residence.

Tenure status of households (type of ownership)

87.   This includes:

-   Household of which a member is the owner of the dwelling;
-   Other forms of tenure.

F. House building cost and prices

88.   The statistics covered by this part of the Programme concern the average house-building costs or prices for a specified unit of measurement (e.g. dwelling, sq. m. of useful floor space etc.). The concepts, definitions and classifications applying to these statistics are set out below and in other parts of the Programme. First, however, the relationship between the concepts of costs, prices and values are considered in general terms.

89.   The term cost is used in the sense of the value of inputs into construction. Total cost is equal to the sum of expenditure on building materials, wages and salaries, and all other expenditure incurred by contractors in connection with the construction work carried out (payments to sub-contractors, etc.) Total cost in respect of a given unit of construction work differs from the value of output, in that the latter includes, in addition, the contractors' profit.

90.   Price refers to the amount paid per unit of output of a defined category of construction work. This unit may be a cubic metre of masonry work, a square metre of roofing, of painting, etc. or a cubic metre of gross volume of a building or even a whole dwelling or building, all of equal quality. The price includes the same elements as those which enter into the calculation of the value of output, and therefore, for a given unit of output, price and value are identical concepts.

91.   In the Programme it is recommended that statistics be compiled on average house-building costs or prices per (i) dwelling, (ii) sq. m. of useful floor space and (iii) cu. mc. of the total volume of residential buildings. In addition, some countries may find it useful to calculate the house-building costs or prices also for other units of measurement, e.g. per room, per sq. m. of living floor space or of gross floor area of the building.

92.   It is recommended to compile these statistics for selected groups of residential buildings, which are uniform from the point of view of size, equipment and technology used in construction. No precise recommendations are included, however, on the specific types of buildings to be taken into account for this purpose since these may vary from country to country depending on the types of building prevailing and technology of construction being used in the country concerned.

93.   For the analysis of variations in house building costs or prices between projects of a given type, it would be desirable to compile data not only on the average costs of prices of buildings of that type, but also data illustrating the variations. This can be done, for instance, by compiling data for the median dwelling and for the upper and lower quartiles.

94.   Average house-building costs or prices per unit of measurement may be determined (in the case of each kind of unit) on the basis of costs or prices of residential buildings completed or of tender prices of projects authorized or begun. When the calculations are based on the costs or prices of residential buildings completed, the results give a picture of the level of costs or prices of dwellings put into use in the period under review. However, average prices calculated on the basis of tender prices of projects authorized or begun do not reflect actual prices on completion of these projects because they cannot take into account changes in projects and in prices during construction. However, they may provide a fairly good basis for analysing the trends of average house-building costs or prices from year to year.

95.   For more detailed analysis of house building costs or prices and of the factors influencing them, countries may wish to make different subdivisions. For instance, the breakdown by different elements of a building, e.g. (i) sub-structure, (ii) super-structure, and (iii) finishing and equipment, would be useful. Such a breakdown would provide inter alia a more adequate basis for analysing the development of house building costs or prices since these may be influenced to a great extent by the costs of the sub-structure, which vary according to site conditions.

96.   Another breakdown of house-building costs or prices which may be of interest for certain purposes is that by cost categories (materials and components, wages and salaries and other costs). Such statistics permit the analysis of the structure of house-building costs and of the different factors by which they are influenced.

97.   As the above-mentioned breakdowns are of national rather than international interest, no specific recommendations concerning them are included in the programme.

98.   Definitions of the units of measurement for which the house building costs or prices may be calculated are as follows:

- dwelling (see para. 45)
- room (see para. 46)
- floor space of a dwelling (see para. 47)

Gross floor area of a building

99.   The gross floor area of a building is the sum of the areas of the stories of the building measured to the outer surface of the outer walls including the area of attics, cellars and communal spaces. Areas of balconies and loggias are excluded. In the case of buildings separated from others by party-walls, the measurement should be made from the centre line of these walls.

Gross volume of a building

100.   The gross volume of a building is the total volume between the outer surface of the outer walls, the level of the lowest floor and the exterior of the roof. When the level of the ground is lower than the lowest floor, the gross volume should be measured from the ground level. In the case of buildings separated from others by party-walls, the measurement should be made from the centre line of these walls.

CHAPTER IV: SOURCES AND METHODS OF COLLECTION

101.   This chapter contains a description and an appraisal of the methods most commonly used in compiling the various statistics included in the Programme.   However, it does not contain definite recommendations, since the appropriate sources and methods depend to a considerable extent on the statistical organization and institutional arrangements in the country concerned. The purpose of this chapter is therefore to give only a general account of the main features of practices in this field, disregarding many detailed differences between countries.

102.   The methods of collection of statistics on the dwelling stock and on the output of housing construction are discussed together, because they are inter-related. Statistical series on the dwelling stock may be compiled from the latest inventory data (housing census) in conjunction with current records on increases and decreases in the dwelling stock. They do not therefore necessarily require periodic collection of data on the dwelling stock as such.

103.   Primary records on increases and decreases in the dwelling stock are kept in most countries by government departments, offices or the local authority organs who are responsible for control of the implementation of housing programmes and policies. Generally, the consent of local authorities is required before the construction of new building or restorations, extensions and conversions or even demolitions can be undertaken. In the application forms for permission to construct or demolish, it is usual to require various types of information which can be used for recording the increases and the losses of dwellings resulting from these activities and for recording the output of housing construction from various aspects. Local authorities

are usually responsible also for identifying dwellings which are unfit for habitation and are also involved in enumerating the extent of damage caused by natural catastrophes. They usually have, therefore, all the information necessary to compile the statistical series on current increases in the dwelling stock and on the output of housing construction.

104.   The basic sources for compiling current statistical series on changes in the dwelling stock and on the output of housing construction are therefore in most countries the applications for authorization to undertake building activity (including demolitions) and records on certain types of decreases in the dwelling stock made by appropriate bodies of local authorities on the spot. However, for maintaining current statistical series on dwellings begun, under construction and completed, the above-mentioned sources should be completed with suitable information on the progress of building work on the projects authorized. This information is either obtained from regular checks on the spot made by the same local authority department as issued the building permit, or is supplied directly by the contractor or the person for whom the house is being built (the investor). In some countries, work completed must be supervised, before the building is declared suitable for habitation, by representatives of the contractor, the investor and usually also the local authority. They draw up a certificate of their conclusions, which usually also contains information which can be used as a source for statistics.

105.   The primary data on the dwelling stock and changes therein, as well as on the output of housing construction, compiled by the local authority organs concerned, are usually submitted directly to the central body responsible for collecting the information on housing in the country as a whole. In a number of countries this is the government department which is charged with formulating and executing housing policy and with coordinating the work of the local authorities in this field. However, in most countries the central statistical authorities are responsible for organizing the statistical work for the country as a whole. In these countries the primary data are collected through regional or district statistical organs (if they exist) which compile the relevant data for both regional and central purposes. There are also countries, where the primary data on the output of housing construction undertaken by public and semi-public bodies are supplied directly by the investors to the Central Statistical Office and/or to the regional statistical organs concerned. However, information on the output of house building construction undertaken by private persons is provided by the local authorities also in these countries.

106.   Whatever the methods of collecting the primary data, the information is submitted on special statistical forms issued by the central body and prescribed for use throughout the country for this purpose. In many countries the above-mentioned statistical forms prescribed for the collection of short-term data (e.g. monthly or quarterly) differ from those used for the collection of statistics at less frequent intervals (e.g. half-yearly or annually). The purpose of the form relating to short-term statistics is usually to make a quick collection of broad information on the output of housing construction without many details. These statistics are mostly a summary of basic information covering all activities in this field of the respective local authority or of investors. The information supplied on the statistical forms for the half yearly or annual data is usually more detailed and is given separately for each building, thus providing a basis for the various classifications of house building output.

107.   The methods of collecting statistical data on changes in dwelling stock and on the output of housing construction described above are used without undue difficulties by countries where the local authorities or other bodies are charged with controlling all housing construction activity (including demolitions) and have the task of following changes in the dwelling stock. However, in a number of countries, authorization to construct or demolish is not needed in certain communes or for certain types of building activity. In these cases the required information does not come directly to the local authorities, and other sources of information therefore need to be used. Some data may be obtained from the firms undertaking the building work or from the credit banks, tax assessors, building material suppliers, health and sanitary inspectors, insurance companies, etc. However, this information is often incomplete and the results are therefore usually

subject to a wider margin of error than in the case of data collected by local authorities. Moreover, the data collected from these sources do not usually allow for the elaboration of classifications needed for current housing policies.

108.   In regard to methods that have been used to collect data on housing conditions, specific recommendations are not included since national circumstances will limit the availability of both sources and methods.

109.   Most countries have some information on housing conditions, principally in regard to the presence of equipment, as part of their regularly scheduled censuses. However the amount of information about housing quality is usually very limited, and because the censuses are generally conducted only once every ten years, that data may not reflect the current housing situation. The collection of such data for intercensal years is also useful.

110.   The other major sources of housing condition statistics are sample surveys and administrative records. Generally, both of these sources have the advantages of more frequent data collection and greater flexibility in content than decennial censuses and the production of summary indicators from these sources for monitoring intercensal changes is useful.

111.   Sample surveys have been used to evaluate housing quality. Some countries have specific surveys designed to measure housing condition while others incorporate housing quality questions as part of a more general housing survey. Differences are also seen in the data source for these surveys. Some attempt to obtain information from a household respondent while others use a professional staff to perform evaluations. Both information sources are valuable. Household respondents are generally aware of the current status of their equipment and at least the gross physical defects in their unit. Professional inspectors can detect and evaluate structural deficiencies, but may lack knowledge on the reliability and adequacy of a household's equipment.

112.   With respect to the collection of information on housing expenditures several sources can be explored. In some countries, the annual budget survey might give appropriate information. Other countries may wish to use household survey results to collect this information or to use a combination of sources.

113.   Most countries collect some information on improvements, repairs and maintenance. The usual sources for these data are household surveys and administrative records. National censuses rarely capture data regarding improvements and repairs.

114.   Household surveys designed to collect data on all family expenditures is a good source of information on housing improvements, repairs and maintenance. Household surveys whose concentration is housing quality could easily incorporate inquiries about recent changes to the dwelling.

115.   A liability of household surveys for this type of data is that when the occupants do not own the dwelling, the owner must be identified and located in order to obtain the vast majority of the expenditure's data. A second contact is also necessary for dwellings where some of the cost for the work is paid by local authorities.

116.   Administrative records may also yield considerable data on improvement, repairs and maintenance, particularly for higher cost work and that which impinges on public health or safety. However, national and even local requirements for reporting work vary. Less expensive jobs and those completed by the dwelling's occupants are likely to be missed in most administrative records.

117.   Methods of compiling statistics on house-building costs vary from country to country depending to considerable extent on the statistical organization and institutional arrangements in the country concerned, and on the sources available for collecting the required data. Different methods, of course, give results of varying reliability. For this reason countries are requested, when publishing the statistics on house-building costs or prices, to describe the methods used.

Table 1:   Number of rooms in a dwelling, number of persons in a household, average size of household

| | TOTAL | SIZE OF HOUSEHOLD (NUMBER OF PERSONS) | | | | | | | | AVERAGE SIZE OF HOUSEHOLD |
		1	2	3	4	5	6	7+	UNKNOWN	
	x 1000									
NUMBER OF ROOMS										
1	.	.	.	.	.	.	.	.	.	.
2	.	.	.	.	.	.	.	.	.	.
3	.	.	.	.	.	.	.	.	.	.
4	.	.	.	.	.	.	.	.	.	.
5	.	.	.	.	.	.	.	.	.	.
6	.	.	.	.	.	.	.	.	.	.
7	.	.	.	.	.	.	.	.	.	.
8+	.	.	.	.	.	.	.	.	.	.
UNKNOWN	.	.	.	.	.	.	.	.		.
TOTAL	.	.	.	.	.	.	.	.		.

Table 2a: Number of persons in a household, useful floor space by tenure

(Number of persons in a household, useful floor space)

(floor space of dwellings measured inside the outer walls, excluding cellars, non-habitual attics and, in multi-dwelling houses, common spaces)

Tenure: owner occupied

| | TOTAL | SIZE OF HOUSEHOLD (NUMBER OF PERSONS) | | | | | | | | AVERAGE SIZE OF HOUSEHOLD |
		1	2	3	4	5	6	7+	UNKNOWN	
	x 1000									
USEFUL FLOOR SPACE (SQ.M.)										
UNDER 50	.	.	.	.	.	.	.	.	.	.
50 TO 75	.	.	.	.	.	.	.	.	.	.
75 TO 100	.	.	.	.	.	.	.	.	.	.
100 TO 125	.	.	.	.	.	.	.	.	.	.
150 TO 175	.	.	.	.	.	.	.	.	.	.
175 TO 200	.	.	.	.	.	.	.	.	.	.
200 TO 225	.	.	.	.	.	.	.	.	.	.
225 TO 250	.	.	.	.	.	.	.	.	.	.
225 TO 250	.	.	.	.	.	.	.	.	.	.
UNKNOWN	.	.	.	.	.	.	.	.	.	.
TOTAL	.	.	.	.	.	.	.	.	.	.

Tenure: others

Idem

Table 2b: Number of persons on a household, living floor space by tenure

(Number of persons in a household, living floor space (the total area of rooms falling under the concept of "room")

Tenure status: owner occupied

	TOTAL	SIZE OF HOUSEHOLD (NUMBER OF PERSONS)								AVERAGE SIZE OF HOUSEHOLD
		1	2	3	4	5	6	7+	UNKNOWN	
LIVING FLOOR SPACE (SQ.M.)	x 1000									
UNDER 50	.	.	.	.	.	.	.	.		.
50 TO 75	.	.	.	.	.	.	.	.		.
75 TO 100	.	.	.	.	.	.	.	.		.
100 TO 125	.	.	.	.	.	.	.	.		.
150 TO 175	.	.	.	.	.	.	.	.		.
175 TO 200	.	.	.	.	.	.	.	.		.
200 TO 225	.	.	.	.	.	.	.	.		.
225 TO 250	.	.	.	.	.	.	.	.		.
225 TO 250	.	.	.	.	.	.	.	.		.
UNKNOWN	.	.	.	.	.	.	.	.		.
TOTAL	.	.	.	.	.	.	.	.		.

Tenure: others

Idem

Table 3: Number of rooms in a dwelling, number of persons in a household, total number of households, by tenure

	TOTAL	SIZE OF HOUSEHOLD (NUMBER OF PERSONS)							
		1	2	3	4	5	6	7+	UNKNOWN
	x 1000								
Owner occupied	.	.	.	.	.	.	.	.	.
Others	.	.	.	.	.	.	.	.	.
TOTAL	.	.	.	.	.	.	.	.	.

Table 4a: Number of rooms in a dwelling, useful space (floor space of dwellings measured inside the outer walls, excluding cellars, non-habitable attics and, in multi- dwelling houses, common spaces)

	TOTAL NUMBER OF DWELLINGS	NUMBER OF ROOMS								
		1	2	3	4	5	6	7	8+	UNKNOWN
	x 1000									
USEFUL FLOOR SPACE (SQ.M.)										
UNDER 50	.	.	.	.	.	.	.	.	.	.
50 TO 75	.	.	.	.	.	.	.	.	.	.
75 TO 100	.	.	.	.	.	.	.	.	.	.
100 TO 125	.	.	.	.	.	.	.	.	.	.
125 TO 150	.	.	.	.	.	.	.	.	.	.
150 TO 175	.	.	.	.	.	.	.	.	.	.
175 TO 200	.	.	.	.	.	.	.	.	.	.
200 TO 225	.	.	.	.	.	.	.	.	.	.
225 TO 250	.	.	.	.	.	.	.	.	.	.
250+	.	.	.	.	.	.	.	.	.	.
UNKNOWN	.	.	.	.	.	.	.	.	.	.
TOTAL	.	.	.	.	.	.	.	.	.	.

Table 4b: Number of rooms in a dwelling, living floor space (the total area of rooms falling under the concept of "room")

	TOTAL NUMBER OF DWELLINGS	NUMBER OF ROOMS								
		1	2	3	4	5	6	7	8+	UNKNOWN
	x 1000									
USEFUL FLOOR SPACE (SQ.M.)										
UNDER 50	.	.	.	.	.	.	.	.	.	.
50 TO 75	.	.	.	.	.	.	.	.	.	.
75 TO 100	.	.	.	.	.	.	.	.	.	.
100 TO 125	.	.	.	.	.	.	.	.	.	.
125 TO 150	.	.	.	.	.	.	.	.	.	.
150 TO 175	.	.	.	.	.	.	.	.	.	.
175 TO 200	.	.	.	.	.	.	.	.	.	.
200 TO 225	.	.	.	.	.	.	.	.	.	.
225 TO 250	.	.	.	.	.	.	.	.	.	.
250+	.	.	.	.	.	.	.	.	.	.
UNKNOWN	.	.	.	.	.	.	.	.	.	.
TOTAL	.	.	.	.	.	.	.	.	.	.

Table 5:   Number of rooms in a dwelling and absence of facilities by tenure

---

Tenure status: owner occupied

	TOTAL NUMBER OF DWELLINGS	NUMBER OF ROOMS								
		1	2	3	4	5	6	7	8+	UNKNOWN
	%									
FACILITIES										
PIPED WATER	.	.	.	.	.	.	.	.	.	.
BATH/SHOWER	.	.	.	.	.	.	.	.	.	.
TOILET	.	.	.	.	.	.	.	.	.	.
CENTRAL HEATING	.	.	.	.	.	.	.	.	.	.
TOTAL	.	.	.	.	.	.	.	.	.	.

Tenure status: others

Idem

Table 6   Number of persons in a household and absence of facilities, by tenure

---

Tenure status: owner occupied

	TOTAL	SIZE OF HOUSEHOLD (NUMBER OF PERSONS)							
		1	2	3	4	5	6	7+	UNKNOWN

---

x 1000

FACILITIES
_____

PIPED WATER	.	.	.	.	.	.	.	.	.
BATH/SHOWER	.	.	.	.	.	.	.	.	.
TOILET	.	.	.	.	.	.	.	.	.
CENTRAL HEATING	.	.	.	.	.	.	.	.	.
TOTAL	.	.	.	.	.	.	.	.	.

Tenure status: others

Idem